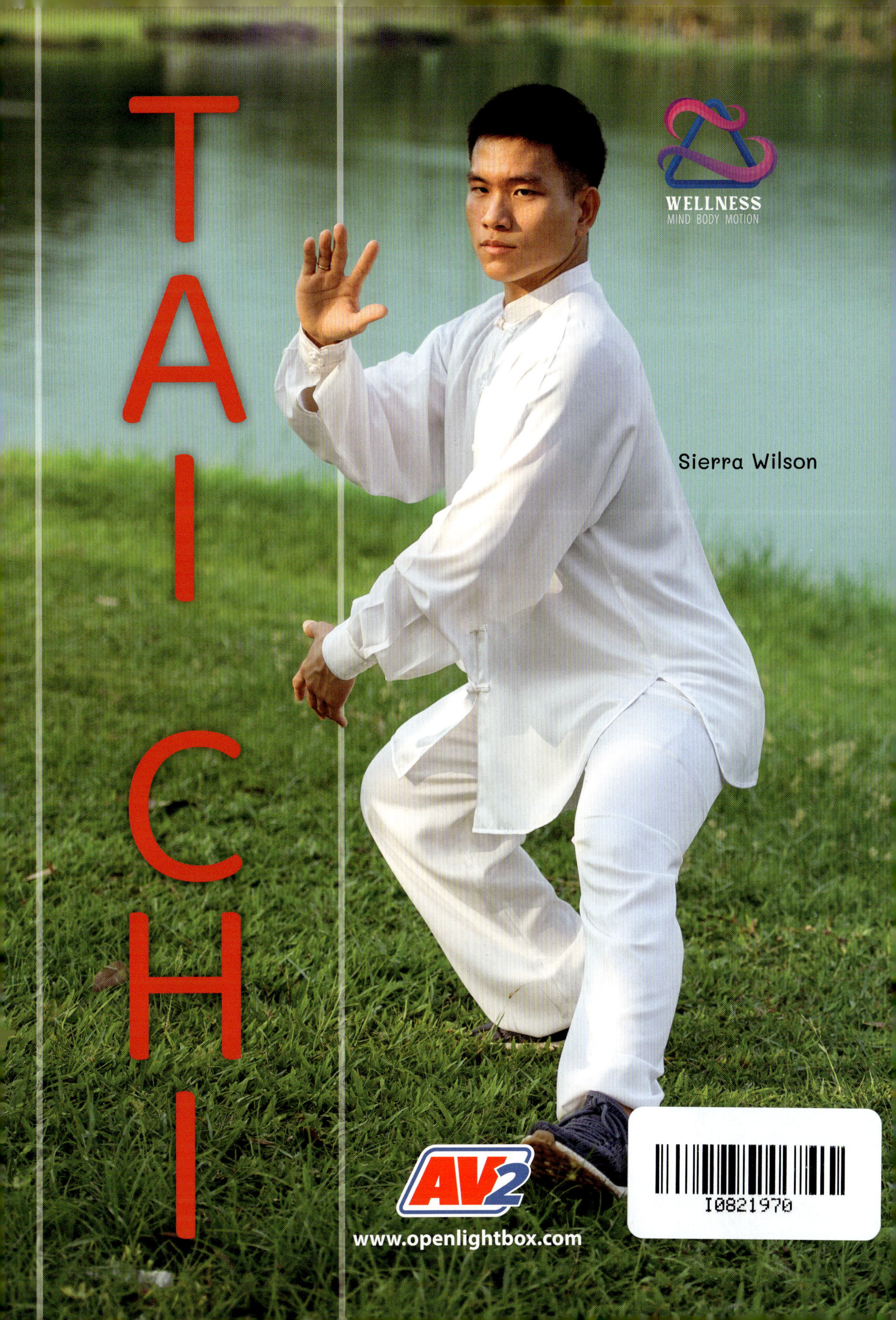
TAI CHI
WELLNESS
MIND BODY MOTION
Sierra Wilson
AV2
www.openlightbox.com
I0821970

Step 1
Go to **www.openlightbox.com**

Step 2
Enter this unique code
DIMYADB09

Step 3
Explore your interactive eBook!

AV2 is optimized for use on any device

Your interactive eBook comes with...

Contents
Browse a live contents page to easily navigate through resources

Audio
Listen to sections of the book read aloud

Videos
Watch informative video clips

Weblinks
Gain additional information for research

Slideshows
View images and captions

Try This!
Complete activities and hands-on experiments

Key Words
Study vocabulary, and complete a matching word activity

Quizzes
Test your knowledge

Share
Share titles within your Learning Management System (LMS) or Library Circulation System

Citation
Create bibliographical references following the Chicago Manual of Style

This title is part of our AV2 digital subscription

1-Year 3–8 Subscription
ISBN 978-1-7911-3306-1

Access hundreds of AV2 titles with our digital subscription.
Sign up for a FREE trial at **www.openlightbox.com/trial**

TAI CHI

2 AV2 Book Code

4 What Is Tai Chi?

6 How It Started

8 Ready for Tai Chi

10 Getting Started

12 Breathe In

14 Flowing Forms

16 Basic Movements

18 Cooling Down

20 The Benefits of Tai Chi

22 Tai Chi Quiz

23 Key Words/Index

What Is Tai Chi?

Tai chi is an ancient Chinese tradition. Today, it is practiced as both a **martial art** and a gentle exercise. It is sometimes referred to as "**meditation** in motion." Tai chi is a popular choice for those who want to find balance between their mind, body, and spirit.

More than **300 million people** practice tai chi **worldwide**.

Tai chi is short for *tai chi chuan*, which means "supreme ultimate fist." Tai chi is connected to ancient Chinese **philosophies** about balance. The goal of tai chi is to allow energy to flow freely and powerfully within a person. To do this, tai chi focuses on slow, flowing movements called forms. These forms are accompanied by deep breathing.

Tai chi is a **low-impact** activity that can be practiced safely by people of all ages. Millions of people around the world practice tai chi to stay healthy and reduce **stress**.

A tai chi practice session is usually **30 to 60 minutes long**.

There are **five major styles** of tai chi.

How It Started

Tai chi began in China hundreds, or possibly thousands, of years ago. According to legend, it was invented by a monk named Chang San-feng. He created tai chi after watching a snake avoid an attacking crane.

Modern tai chi probably started in China's Chen village. The Chen villagers held the secrets of tai chi closely. However, in the 1800s, a young man named Yang Lu Chan entered the village. He posed as a servant in order to secretly learn tai chi. Yang studied for many years before being discovered. A Chen master recognized Yang's dedication and took him on as an apprentice for 18 years. Afterward, Yang became a well-known teacher. He developed his own style of tai chi, also called Yang. As time went on, other styles of tai chi developed, including Hao, Wu, and Sun.

Yang Lu Chan

Tai chi first came to the United States in the 1930s, when a Chinese immigrant named Choy Hok Peng began teaching it in San Francisco. It did not gain widespread popularity until 1954. This was when dancer Sophia Delza gave a tai chi demonstration in New York City's Museum of Modern Art.

Timeline

12th century BC The beliefs behind tai chi are mentioned in the *Book of Changes*, or *I Ching*, an important, ancient Chinese text.

400 AD Monks in China's Shaolin Temple learn an 18-movement tai chi-style exercise.

About 1670 Chen Wangting begins developing the Chen style of tai chi.

About 1820 Yang Lu Chan starts secretly studying tai chi in the Chen Village.

1961 The first English-language book on tai chi is published. It is written by Sophia Delza.

2020 In recognition of its value to people all over the world, tai chi is added to **UNESCO**'s Representative List of the Intangible Cultural Heritage of Humanity.

Ready for Tai Chi

People can practice tai chi almost anywhere and at anytime. It can be practiced alone or in groups, outdoors or indoors. Practicing tai chi outdoors can help students connect with nature and feel calmer. However, the benefits of tai chi are best achieved with regular practice and a commitment to its **principles**.

Equipment

Tai chi does not require much equipment. All people need is a flat, open area. Still, some equipment can help add comfort and variety to the tai chi experience.

Loose Clothing

Although tai chi can be practiced in any clothing, loose, comfortable clothing is best. Many students choose to wear a T-shirt and sweatpants. Others wear more traditional martial arts clothing. Loose clothing allows for freely flowing movements.

Water Bottle

As with all physical activity, **hydration** is important. Keeping a water bottle nearby allows students to focus on tai chi without becoming thirsty or needing to leave class.

Shoes

In some situations, tai chi can be practiced barefoot. In others, it is safer to wear shoes to protect the feet. Flat shoes, such as tennis shoes or martial arts shoes, work best. Heeled shoes should be avoided because they affect balance.

Traditional Weapons

As tai chi is a martial art, it can be practiced with traditional Chinese weapons. These can include the broad sword and the pole. Weapons can help students learn to control and extend their energy. Usually, students do not begin using weapons until after studying weapons-free tai chi.

Getting Started

Tai chi classes often start with relaxation. Students sit or stand in a circle with their eyes closed as the teacher leads the class through breathing and meditation exercises. This is a time to calm the mind and prepare for the class to come. Tai chi is about both the body and the mind. The start of class focuses on the mind.

After relaxation, students begin gentle warm-ups to ready the body for tai chi forms. Warm-ups include simple motions such as swaying and shoulder rolls. These movements loosen the muscles and **joints** that will be used later in class.

When warm-up exercises are completed, students spread out to learn forms. Students need enough space to fully extend their limbs in all directions. The teacher will demonstrate movements while the students follow along. Sometimes, advanced students assist beginning students.

After certain movements have been learned, students are taught a pattern of breathing to match each movement. They are also shown how to focus on the flow of their energy. Even simple tai chi forms require plenty of practice. The more students practice, the better they become at connecting their movements in a smooth, flowing way.

Etiquette in a Tai Chi Class

A tai chi class is meant to be focused, peaceful, and respectful. Show respect to your teachers and other students by arriving early, doing your best, and following instructions. Turn off your phone, and avoid conversations during class sessions. Mastering tai chi takes time, so remember to be patient with yourself and others.

Breathe In

Mindful breathing is a key part of tai chi. It requires people to focus on the rhythm and flow of their breathing. Tai chi breathing should feel calm and natural, with **inhaling** and **exhaling** matching the flow of the tai chi movements.

Breathing exercises are a great way to relax and release stress. You can practice mindful breathing at home or anywhere you like.

Try mindful breathing for yourself.

1. Sit in a chair or stand up straight.
2. Breathe out until you feel the need to take a deep breath in. Keep your tongue touching the roof of your mouth as you breathe.
3. Try to breathe only through your nose. Keep your breathing continuous, with no pause between inhaling and exhaling. Make sure to breathe deep into your **abdomen**.
4. As you inhale, move your hands apart. As you exhale, bring them back together.
5. Continue breathing in this way for several minutes and pay attention to how you feel.
6. Next time you feel anxious or stressed, try mindful breathing, and see if you notice your body and mind become calmer.

Flowing Forms

Much of a tai chi class is spent learning and practicing forms. These are often taught in sets. Some sets are short, with only a dozen or so movements. Others are long, sometimes with more than 100 movements.

Tai chi can have as many as **108 separate movements**.

In **2017,** England's **Sheila Dickinson** set the record for the **longest** tai chi **marathon,** at **28 hours** and **59 minutes**.

Each style of tai chi teaches forms differently. Yang style, the most popular, is graceful, slow, and gentle. Wu style focuses on smaller movements. Although Chen is the original tai chi style, it is now practiced by only a few. Instead of focusing only on slow movements, Chen style combines slow movements with fast ones. The Hao style is mainly practiced in China. It uses subtle movements and is focused more on the flow of energy inside the body. The Sun style is known for its detailed footwork and flowing hand motions. Combination styles use movements from many different tai chi styles, as well as other martial arts.

In 2015, **53,803 people** did tai chi at the **same time** in China's Jiaozuo City, setting a **world record** for the largest martial arts display in multiple venues.

Basic Movements

Beginner tai chi forms use only a few movements. These simpler forms help introduce students to the flowing motions of tai chi. Learning simple forms can help build skills and confidence. To get started, try practicing these short tai chi forms.

Flying Wild Goose

This form is a gentle exercise for the wrists and shoulders. Imagine that you are a strong, majestic goose in flight.

1. Stand with your feet shoulder-width apart. Balance your weight evenly on both legs.
2. Breathe in.
3. Lean forward to feel your weight in the balls of your feet.
4. Lift your arms out and up like flapping wings. Keep your arms relaxed and your palms facing down.
5. Bend your wrists until your palms face away from you on each side.
6. Breathe out.
7. Lower your arms and sink down, bending both knees.

Scooping from the Sea

As you complete this form, imagine that you are gathering water from the sea and lifting it high over your head before letting it rain down on you.

1. Stand with your left foot in front of you and left knee bent. Shift your weight slightly to the left side.
2. Breathe in.
3. Bend forward at your waist and bring your hands in front of you. Stack your hands with the palms facing up.
4. Bring your hands up over your head. Slowly separate your hands and shift your weight back to your right foot. Breathe out.
5. Open your arms wide, and bend forward to scoop again.
6. Repeat this move with the right foot forward.

Carrying the Moon

Imagine holding the full moon as you twist from side to side. This form is a gentle way to exercise your back.

1. Stand with your feet shoulder-width apart. Breathe in.
2. Twist from the waist toward your left side, keeping your shoulders relaxed and your arms slightly bent.
3. Reach both arms back toward your left side as though you are twisting and holding the moon.
4. Keep your eyes on your hands. Breathe out.
5. Lower your hands, return to a forward-facing position, and repeat on the right side.

Cooling Down

Even though tai chi is calm and peaceful, it is still hard work. Ending a tai chi session with a cool-down routine helps lower the heart rate and adds another layer of relaxation. A cool-down can also be a time to reflect on things learned in class and how your body feels.

Cool-down exercises are gentler and easier than the forms that make up the middle of a tai chi class. Students may complete a standing exercise, raising and lowering the arms and slightly bending, as if washing the body with energy from head to toe. They may also scoop the arms in and out toward a spot just below the belly button called the *dan tien*, or center of gravity in the body. As they do this, students focus on gathering energy while breathing in and out.

As the class winds down, the students may rest their hands on their dan tien and focus on breathing. This is a type of standing meditation. It gives students time to relax and feel calm. At the end of class, students may show respect by bowing.

The Benefits of Tai Chi

Tai chi practice brings many benefits to the body and mind. The full-body movements used in many tai chi forms help to strengthen the arm, leg, and **core muscles**. Regular practice builds strength and flexibility. Tai chi also improves balance. In fact, studies show that tai chi can lower the risk of falling for older adults. Other studies show that tai chi helps with maintaining a healthy weight and healthy **cholesterol** levels. Some other health benefits of tai chi can include more energy, lower blood pressure, a stronger immune system, and less joint pain.

As tai chi also focuses on the mind, it can help mental health. Tai chi can lower stress. It can also improve mood.

The best way to get the full health benefits of tai chi is through regular practice. At least 20 to 30 minutes of tai chi per day are recommended. However, any amount of tai chi practice is better than none. The calming principles, breathing **techniques**, and meditation skills learned through tai chi can be used anytime, anywhere.

Tai chi is said to follow the **70 percent rule**. It states that by giving 70 percent effort instead of 100 percent, a person stays **calmer** and **achieves more**.

Created in the **1980s**, mulan quan is the **only style of tai chi** designed exclusively for **women**.

Approximately 5 million people in the United States practice tai chi for its mind-body benefits.

Tai Chi Quiz

1. What does *tai chi chuan* mean?
2. How many major styles of tai chi exist today?
3. In what country did tai chi begin?
4. What kind of clothing is best for tai chi practice?
5. Which tai chi style is the most popular?
6. Which tai chi style is the original?
7. Which basic tai chi form involves moving the arms like wings?
8. What is the dan tien?
9. How does tai chi affect mental health?
10. What is the only tai chi style designed exclusively for women?

ANSWERS

1. "Supreme ultimate fist" **2.** Five **3.** China **4.** Loose, comfortable clothing **5.** Yang style **6.** Chen style **7.** Flying Wild Goose **8.** A spot just below the belly button, the body's center of gravity **9.** It lowers stress and improves mood. **10.** Mulan quan

Key Words

abdomen: muscles in the stomach area

cholesterol: a waxy substance in the body

core muscles: major muscles that move and support the spine, and keep it stable

exhaling: breathing out

hydration: having enough water in the body

inhaling: breathing in

joints: points in the body where two bones connect, such as knees and elbows

low-impact: putting low amounts of pressure on the body's joints

martial art: a traditional form of self-defense

meditation: mental exercises done for the purpose of calming the mind or reaching spiritual awareness

mindful: conscious or aware of something

philosophies: sets of beliefs or values

principles: fundamental concepts or ideas

stress: a state of mental or emotional strain

techniques: special ways of doing an activity

UNESCO: the United Nations Educational, Scientific and Cultural Organization, which promotes world peace and security through international cooperation

Index

Chang San-feng 6
Chen style 6, 7, 15, 22
China 6, 7, 15, 22
Choy Hok Peng 6
combination styles 15

dan tien 19, 22
Delza, Sophia 6, 7

equipment 9

forms 5, 10, 11, 14, 15, 16, 17, 19, 20, 22

Hao style 6, 15

mindful breathing 12, 13
Mulan quan style 21, 22

Sun style 6, 15

weapons 9
Wu style 6, 15

Yang Lu Chan 6, 7
Yang style 6, 15, 22

Published by Lightbox Learning
276 5th Avenue, Suite 704 #917
New York, NY 10001
Website: www.openlightbox.com

Library of Congress Cataloging-in-Publication Data
Names: Wilson, Sierra, author.
Title: Tai chi / Sierra Wilson.
Description: New York, NY : AV2, 2022. | Series: Wellness : mind body motion | Includes index. | Audience: Grades 2-3
Identifiers: LCCN 2021033632 (print) | LCCN 2021033633 (ebook) | ISBN 9781791142629 (library binding) | ISBN 9781791142636 (paperback) | ISBN 9781791142643
Subjects: LCSH: Tai chi for children--Juvenile literature. | Mindfulness (Psychology)--Juvenile literature.
Classification: LCC GV504.6.C44 W55 2022 (print) | LCC GV504.6.C44 (ebook) | DDC 796.815/5083--dc23
LC record available at https://lccn.loc.gov/2021033632
LC ebook record available at https://lccn.loc.gov/2021033633

Printed in Guangzhou, China
1 2 3 4 5 6 7 8 9 0 25 24 23 22 21

092021
101120

Editor Heather Kissock
Designer Terry Paulhus

Photo Credits
Every reasonable effort has been made to trace ownership and to obtain permission to reprint copyright material. The publisher would be pleased to have any errors or omissions brought to its attention so that they may be corrected in subsequent printings. Lightbox Learning acknowledges Getty Images, Alamy, Shutterstock, Dreamstime, and Wikimedia Commons as its primary photo suppliers for this title.